Management Accounting

The Ultimate Guide to Managerial
Accounting for Beginners Including
Management Accounting Principles

Contents

Introduction

What is the value of your business or company? That is a great question. Many business owners do not know their company's value. I want to take the time to give you the tools to find out yours. It is essential that you know how much your business is worth.

Welcome to the joys of management accounting. When you really think about it, the name says it all. This form of accounting is designed for the management level. Through the combination of accounting, finance and management you will be equipped with the business skills and techniques needed to add real value to your organization.

When you have someone working for your business who is highly trained in management accounting, then you have someone who can do it all and truly help you thrust your business to success.

Throughout this book, you will get valuable insights into the superman of accounting; the management accountant. As we research what management accounting has in store, it is important to note the impact this will have on your business. I am not referring to negative impacts, either.

When you have a management accountant, you have a superhero in the company. They do it all when it comes to the management aspect of running your business. Keep reading and you will find out exactly what I am talking about.

But we're not going to stop there. Perhaps you are a management accountant, thinking of becoming one, or will be hiring someone who is proficient in the field. If so, the last chapter is for you. I want you to know what types of jobs there are out there and the ins and outs of them.

Chapter 1 – Management Accounting and Its Importance

Before I can start to take you on tour into management accounting, you first need to know what it is and why it is important to your business. I posed a question in the introduction, "What is the value of your business or company?" This is the type of question you can answer through management accounting.

Through this accounting, we can source, analyze, communicate and use decision-relevant financial and non-financial information to generate and preserve value for your company. We can combine accounting, finance, and management with the business skills and techniques you will need for adding this value.

You heard me state that a management accountant is like a superhero to the company. This is due to the ability to work across the business and not just within finance. They can advise managers of financial implications of their big decisions, formulate business strategies and monitor the risk. They can do more than just crunch numbers. They can help you run your business as a team that will be unstoppable. They use more than the financial information. Instead, they will use data from across the board to lead and inform the management of business strategies and drive the company to sustainable success.

You will find management accountants working in a wide variety of jobs such as finance, IT, marketing, HR, operations and senior management positions. This is only a small list as they could be found in any position imaginable.

Keep in mind: there are some differences between financial accounting and management accounting.

- ➤ **Financial Accounting:**
    - ○ They will prepare reports that are generally based on the past performances. These reports will be in line with all reporting requirements.
    - ○ They will produce the required financial information for use by the other functions throughout your business. A good example will be information that will be used by the department managers.

- ➤ **Management Accounting:**
    - ○ They will collate information such as the revenue, cash flow and any outstanding debts. This information will produce timely trend reports and statistics to inform important, day-to-day management and business decisions. These reports and statistics are also done through management accounting.
    - ○ They will combine the financial information with your nonfinancial information for them to paint a complete picture of your business. They will use this information to drive your business to success.

Management accounting is a profession that will involve partnering in the management decision making, devising planning, and performance management systems, providing expertise in financial reporting and control and assist management in the formation of your business. In a nutshell, management accounting is typically considered one of the members of management and helps to guide your business into the future. The main role of management accounting will be in budgeting.

Granted, as a business owner there is one question that is probably on your mind, "How can I use managerial accounting to make it effectively work for my business?" This question will soon be answered throughout this book.

Management accounting is the process of identifying, analyzing, recording and presenting your financial information. This is the information you can use internally by the management for planning, decision making, and control. With management accounting, you are equipped with a tool that has a process for preparing management reports and accounts with accurate and timely financial and statistical information to your managers. This valuable information will help in making short and long-term decisions for your business.

I mentioned that the main role of management accounting is budgeting. However, the basic objective is to assist the management in performing all their functions effectively. That means, a management accountant will assist in the planning, organizing, directing and controlling of your business.

Before we can dive into management accounting, it is important that we know the tools and techniques that are available and used by management accountants.

➢ Financial Planning (This is considered a main objective of any business organization for you to maximize your profits)
➢ Financial Statement Analysis
➢ Cost Accounting
➢ Fund Flow Analysis
➢ Cash Flow Analysis
➢ Standard Costing
➢ Marginal Costing
➢ Budgetary Control

This is only a short list of the tools available to a managerial accountant. The typical job description for a management accountant includes:

> ➢ Certain reports need to be prepared, the budgets will need to be created and maintained and all the major financial statements will need to be obtained from the business.

> ➢ You will be asked to perform duties within our financial admin section that will help the process of performing audits internally.

> ➢ You will be expected to create a relationship with our management and its staff to include everyone you work with.

> ➢ Supervising a team of accounting technicians.

> ➢ You will be expected to develop our business financial system and all the policies including managing them once they are established.

The Roles of Management Accounting in Your Organization

I have briefly mentioned some of the roles in management accounting. These gave you a small glance into what it is all about. Now we will focus more on the specific areas as we venture into the very deeps of management accounting.

Helping Forecast the Future: Every business owner is looking for a fortune teller to provide information on what the future has in store for their business. With the help of forecasting, we have a fortune teller. Much like a real fortune teller, this will not be 100% accurate. However, through management accounting that accuracy is a lot better with forecasting than a fortune teller can offer. This will be a great aid in making decisions and answering valuable questions. These questions could include:

> ➢ Should my business invest in more equipment?

> Should I diversify into different markets?

> Should I buy another company?

With management accounting, you will now have the answers to these critical questions with your forecasts and consider the future trends of your business. These are only a select few of many questions you may have and now have the answers for.

Helping in Make-or-Buy Decisions: Ask yourself, "Will it be cheaper to produce materials and obtain a product from a third party or to manufacture them in-house? The cost and production availability will become a valuable deciding factor in the choices you make as a business owner. Through management accounting, you now have useful insights that can enable the decision-making at both the operational and strategic levels.

Forecasting Cash Flow: Having enough cash flow within your business is essential for its survival. It's also of vital importance to have the ability to predict your cash flow. Through the forecasting of your cash flow, you can answer questions such as:

> How much cost will the company incur in the future?

> Where will its revenues come from and will the revenues increase or decrease in the future?

Management accounting will involve designing your budgets and trend charts. Your managers will use this information to decide how they need to allocate the money and resources for them to generate the projected revenue growth. In a way, this will set a goal for your management team.

Helping Understand Performance Variances: Understanding this is half the battle most business owners and managers must overcome to see great success. Your business performance discrepancies are variances between what was predicted and achieved. With management accounting, we can use analytical techniques that will help your management build on the positive variances and manage the negatives ones.

Analyzing the Rate of Return: Before you embark on a project that will require heavy investments, you must analyze the expected rate of return (ROR). If you are given two or more investment opportunities, ask yourself:

> ➤ How should my company choose the most profitable one?

> ➤ How many years would it take for my company to break even on the project?

> ➤ What are the cash flows for the project likely going to be?

These are all vital questions that management accounting will provide the answers to.

Tools of Management Accounting: This is an area that I feel is so important that we will discuss them in further detail in their own chapter. For now, I want you to be aware of the tools that will be available to you. These wonderful tools are essential for forecasting your business trends.

> ➤ Ratios

> ➤ Skills and ability to read and analyze financial statements

> ➤ Management information systems (MIS)

> ➤ Key performance indicators (KPIs)

> ➤ Simulations

> ➤ Financial modeling

> ➤ The Balanced Scorecard

> ➤ Any other set of data that your company can produce for a complete analysis

Management accounting will find answers to those hard-integral questions that your senior management can use to focus on maximizing your revenues.

I have seen businesses fail because they did not have the tools for success. Management accounting has transformed how companies operate. These decisions that drive your business needs to consider the implications and outcomes of what the future holds for your company. Through using intelligent analysis and management accounting, you can now make smart decisions that will ensure a prosperous future and growth for your business.

Objectives and Functions of Management Accounting

The fundamental objective of management accounting is to help your management make quality decisions for controlling your business activities. Think of it like this; you have a primary goal. This goal is long-term. The question is; how will you achieve this long-term goal? The answer is simple. You make several short-term goals that will be geared toward the achievement of your long-term goal. Now you will get objectives and functions that will act as the short-term goals and help you achieve your long-term goal or main objective.

Presentation of Data: Presentation is everything. When we look at the typical profit and loss account and the balance sheet; what information can you use for making decisions? In short, both are not useful for decision-making in accounting. This means the information needs to be modified and re-arranged in such a manner so it will help your management in making decisions through the various techniques.

Modifies Data: Financial reports are great in providing valuable information about the finances of your business from month-to-month. Even though this is still great information, it does not provide the essential information your management needs. That means we need to modify this information according to the expectations of your management. For example, you have the total purchase figures. These figures will need to be modified to show monthly income, amounts per each product, the suppliers with all financial information and the territory for your products.

Forecasting: You have probably noticed that forecasting is a function and a role of management accounting. That is because it is an important area that is provided through this accounting. Your management can forecast the achievement of your objectives for short-term and long-term goals. Your management accountant will provide all the necessary information and data you need for these forecasts.

Analysis and Interpretation of Data: It was already mentioned that your financial statements will need to be rearranged. This also needs to happen for the proper analysis to be performed. Comparative and common size statements are prepared for the meaningful interpretation of your data. You will see ratios performed and calculated to give you the projected trends.

Help in Organizing: Take a moment to think about what it means to organize your business. What is involved within this organization and how can management accounting assist with this organization? With management accounting, you will have help in allocating your companies resources to the various departments and the assignment of duties to your employees at the various management levels. The modified data, analysis and interpretations will help in keeping your management organized.

Means of Communication: Communication is essential for any business. The analysis and interpretation of your modified data are conveyed to your employees. The more meaningful information is supplied to all levels of management. In this way, modified data is used as a means of communication through the management accounting system.

Planning: This is a vital area that needs to be addressed. Ask yourself what you can do with the information from the fund flow statement, cash flow statement, budgeting, standard costing, capital budgeting and marginal costing information. All this information is essential for planning.

Facilitates Control: Management accounting will translate the objectives into achievements within a specific time. This is possible through budgetary control and standard costing which will be an integral part of management accounting. So in conclusion, management accounting will facilitate control.

Decision-Making: As a business owner and through your management team, decision-making is essential. Modified data, analysis and interpreted information are highly useful to your management. It will give them the ability to make quality decisions and policy information through the management accounting system.

Use of Qualitative Information: Employees efficiency, policies of your management and employer/employee relationships are examples of qualitative information. They cannot rely on measures in terms of rupees, units, kilograms and tons. These types of information are used by your management accounting system.

Coordination: The preparation of budgets on a functional basis will be the fixation of targets for each of your separate departments. The objectives of your organization will be achieved through attainment of targets of all your departments. The preparation of periodical performance reports of all your departments will be under the management accounting system and will bring coordination among all your departments.

Special Cost and Economic Studies: Within the management accounting system we will consider the special cost and economic studies to increase your profits that are of concern.

Accountability: Management accounting lays great emphasis on accountability through effective performance measures. By setting targets for strategic business units and your departments, management accounting can be an asset in the assignment of responsibility for the achievement of your business targets by your individual managers. Responsibility accounting will be achieved by appraising the performance of managers responsible for your business units while giving due consideration to factors not within their control or influence.

Motivating Employees: Your employees need to be motivated to perform at their best. The preparation of budgets and the adoption of standard costing techniques automatically do just that in an indirect way. If your budgets are achieved, and there are any variances under the standard costing techniques, a suitable monetary and non-monetary motivating scheme can be prepared and implemented. For example, you may find extra room within the budget to offer an all-expense paid trip to the Philippines to your employees or a Christmas bonus to help their families during the holidays.

Major Limitations of Management Accounting

Like with everything, there are some limitations to management accounting. These limitations can be overcome through extra training. However, they do exist if you are solely relying on the accounting system only. Here are a few limitations to be aware of with this system:

Based on Records: When you use management accounting, you will take into consideration the past records that are provided by the financial and cost accounting when making your decisions for the future. The accuracy and utility of these past records will limit the dependence of the management accountant for the future decisions. If your past data is not reliable, your decisions that are suggested by your management accountant will be misleading.

Lack of Knowledge and Understanding of the Related Subjects: For management to make sound business decisions it is crucial they have knowledge of various fields such as accounting, statistics, economics, taxation, production, engineering and more. However, it has been observed that the individual who makes the decisions may not have a comprehensive knowledge of all the subjects they are associated with.

Intuitive Decisions: It has been realized that scientific decisions must take into consideration the quantitative techniques. However, due to the simplicity and personal factors, the management has a tendency for intuitive decision-making.

Lack of Continuity and Coordination: For your management accountant's conclusions to be meaningful, they must be implemented into your business at the various levels. Typically, they lose their significance because it is not feasible to implement such conclusions.

No Substitute of Administration: The techniques and tools that are suggested by your management accountant are not alternatives or substitutes of a good administration. In fact, they are only used to supplement the sound management and administration.

Lack of Objectivity: From the collection of data to the interpretation stage in the financial accounting, there is always a possibility of personal bias and manipulation. Which means, it will lose objectivity and validity.

Unquantifiable Variables: There are many problems in a business that cannot be expressed in momentary terms. These problems cannot be interpreted for the future.

Costly: A management accounting system requires a large organization and a wide network of rules and regulations that will have a considerable investment needed for its implementation. That means it cannot be utilized by a small organization and still have an immediate profit.

Not in Final Stage: Management accounting is still a baby. That means it has not reached its final stage and is still being developed. That is the main reason why the techniques suffer from the fluidity of concepts, diversity in opinions and various interpretations.

Psychological Resistance: For you to introduce and operate a management accounting system in your organization, it will require a lot of changes in your organization's structure, rules and regulations. The management itself may resist these changes as it creates difficulties in its successful operations.

Many of these limitations can be overcome through training, while others can be worked through as new systems are incorporated into your business to pick up the slack from the limitations of the management accounting system.

Chapter 2 – Management Accounting Principles

All forms of accounting have specific principles associated to them. The same goes for management accounting. The purpose of these principles will be to support your organization through benchmarking and improving your management accounting system. They will aid in helping your business make better decisions, respond appropriately to risks, and to protect the value you will generate.

Designing and Compiling: Accounting information, records, reports, statements and other evidence of past, present or future results should be designed and compiled to meet the needs of your business or problem.

Your management accounting system will be designed to present relevant data. The information of your financial statements can be modified to meet the requirements of your management.

Management by Exception: This principle will be followed when presenting information to your management. It means that budgetary control systems and the standard costing techniques are followed in the management accounting system. The performance is compared with pre-determined ones to find deviations. The unfavorable deviations are then given to the management so improvements can be made.

Control at Source Accounting: The costs are best controlled at the point where they incurred. For example, individual performance of your employee can be prepared in the form of quantitative and qualitative information. Thus, control can be exercised over your employees.

Accounting for Inflation: A profit cannot be said to be earned unless capital is maintained intact in real terms, which means that the value of money is not stable. It is necessary to assess the value of capital contributed by you, the owner, in terms of real value of money through the revaluation accounting. The rate of inflation is considered to judge the real success of your business concerns.

Use of Return on Investment: This is also known as Return on Capital Employed. The rate of return will show the efficiency of your business concern. For this purpose, the capital employed is calculated in terms of real money value.

Utility: Your management accounting system and its related forms should be used only if they serve a useful purpose.

Integration: All the required information of your management is integrated so they can be used effectively at the maximum and at the same time the accounting service is provided at the minimum cost.

Absorption of Overhead Costs: Your overhead costs are absorbed on any of the predetermined bases. These costs are a combination of indirect materials, indirect labor and indirect expenses. Which means the selected method for the absorption of overhead should bring the desired results in the most equitable manner.

Utilization of Resources: The available resources should be used effectively. The reason is that some of your resources are available in plenty while some of your other resources are scarce throughout the year. Your management accounting system should ensure the proper utilization of your available resources.

Controllable and Uncontrollable Costs: Based on the controllability of costs, you will see two types in which they are classified. These types are controllable and uncontrollable. There is no meaning in taking steps to control the uncontrollable costs. There are techniques for you to control the uncontrollable costs through your management accounting system.

Forward-Looking Approach: Your management accounting system can guess the future problems through the standard costing techniques through the means of a fixed standard, which will allow for the problems to possibly be prevented.

Appropriate Means: You will want to use the most appropriate means of accumulating, recording and presenting the accounting information. For example, you would use an ordinary computer for a small business while a large corporation would use an advanced technology computer with the proper software.

Personal Contacts: Your personal contact with the departmental managers, foreman and others cannot be replaced completely by reports and statements. That means when you have direct personal contact you can avoid the misunderstanding between your management and employees.

Even though we have a pretty good list of principles, there are a few I want to focus our attention to. These principles could change your business and point you in the right direction for success. These principles alone can bring structure to a business that may be in chaos. Here they are:

Influence *(Communication provides insight that is influential)*: Your management accounting will begin and end with conversations. It will improve your decision-making by communicating some insightful information through all stages of the decision-making process. Anyone who has a business knows the importance of good communication. This critical information will allow your management accounting to cut silos and facilitate the integrated thinking. The consequences of the actions in one area of your business onto another area of your business can be better understood, accepted or repaired. When you communicate and discuss the needs of the decision-makers, the most relevant information can be sourced and analyzed, making their decisions useful and achieving influence within your business.

Relevance *(Information is relevant)*: With your management accounting we can scan the best available resources for information that is relevant to the decision that needs to be taken, the person making the decision and the decision style or process that is being used. It is important to understand the needs of your stakeholders. When you understand their needs, the most relevant information for decision-making is identified, collected and prepared for analysis. Relevance requires achieving an appropriate balance between the following:

> ➤ Past, present and future-related information

> ➤ Internal and external information

> ➤ Financial and nonfinancial information, including environmental and social issues

Value *(Impact on Value is Analyzed)*: Management accounting will connect your business strategies to your business model which will require a thorough understanding of the macroeconomic environment. This will involve analyzing your information along the value-generation path, evaluating opportunities and focusing on the risks, costs and value-generation of your potential opportunities. Through scenario analysis, you can bring a rigor for evaluating your business decisions.

Trust *(Stewardship Builds Trust)*: Through accountability and scrutiny, you can make your decision-making process more objective. Balancing your short-term commercial interests against your long-term value for your stakeholders will enhance the creditability and trust of your business. Your management accountant is trusted to be ethical, accountable and mindful of your business values, governance requirements and social responsibilities.

Knowing these principles is one thing. However, knowing when to apply them will send your business into success. Keep in mind, to effectively use these principles; three factors will play a major role in the effective application of the last four principles.

Understanding the Need: The appreciation that your management accounting system can help your business achieve sustainable success. The test for each principle is its ability to contribute to the success of your business.

Tools and Techniques: In the practical application of the principles, you need to use the appropriate tools and techniques. These tools and techniques must be adapted and continually refined as objective changes.

Diagnostic: People skills, principles, practice areas and performance management systems can help your business assess the effectiveness of your management accounting functions and identify areas that may need improvement.

I do understand that this is a lot to take in at once. These principles can help you see a successful future. Granted, after these factors are considered you can use the four principles at the end and apply them to 13 key practice areas of your management accounting system.

1. Cost transformation and management
2. External reporting
3. Financial strategy
4. Internal control
5. Investment appraisal
6. Management and budgetary control
7. Price, discount and product decision
8. Product management
9. Regulatory adherence and compliance

10. Resource management

11. Risk management

12. Strategic tax management

13. Treasury and cash management

There's one more area to consider even though it is not technically part of management accounting. These guidance's can also be applied to internal audit. Keep in mind: your management accounting makes a significant contribution to the system of internal controls as it is tested and appraised by the internal audit functions.

Chapter 3 – Responsibility Accounting

What comes to your mind when you hear about responsibility accounting? I want you to take a moment and think about it. Consider this: you can go off the assumption that every cost that is incurred must be the responsibility of one person somewhere in the company. As you use this approach, your cost reports can be tailored for each recipient. However, as you move upward through your organization structure, it will be common to find fewer responsibility reports being used. Now ask yourself, "do we still need to use these reports through the entire organization at all levels, or are there some areas that may not need them?" This is a question that only one can answer as the decision-making process continues. However, to see great success, you should continue to use these reports at all levels of the structure.

I want to approach the original question; what is responsibility accounting? This accounting will involve your company's internal accounting and your budgeting. The objective is to assist in the planning and controlling processes of your company's responsibility centers such as decentralizing your departments and divisions. Usually, this will involve the preparation of your annual and monthly budgets for each of your responsibility centers. Thus, classifying the actual transactions by your responsibility centers and preparing a monthly report. These reports will present the actual amounts for each budget line item to include the variance between the budget and actual amounts. This will allow for your company and each manager of your responsibility center to receive feedback on the manager's performance each month.

In short, your responsibility accounting will be your system which will involve pinpointing your responsibility centers and their objectives, developing performance measurements schemes, and preparing and analyzing performance reports of the responsibility centers. This will involve reporting and gathering your costs and revenues by each area of responsibility.

Advantages of Having Responsibility Accounting

There are three core advantages with responsibility accounting.

Responsibility Accounting and the Delegates Decision Making: Supervisors, department heads and line managers are imposed with your operational decisions. Your top management such as the executives can focus on the long-term, or strategic, objectives.

It Will Provide a Guide for an Evaluation of Performance: This will help create the standards where they will be used as a comparison against the actual results.

It will promote **Management by Exception** and **Management by Objectives**.

> ➤ **Management by Objectives:** This will be a path where your managers will agree on a set of objectives and goals which brings us to why it is called management by objective. This performance of your managers and their subordinates are to be evaluated according to their achievements of the goals.

> ➤ **Management by Exception:** This is another approach where your management will give their attention to the matters that will drift from the established standard. As an example, when you have a department with an extremely high cost that is

compared to the amount you budgeted for, your management shall focus on figuring out why the high costs and fix the major concerns by perhaps cutting the costs, establishing new standards or press re-engineering.

It may not seem easy to implement responsibility accounting. In fact, three areas must be followed to implement responsibility accounting effectively.

1. You will need a structure that is well-defined within your organization. The responsibility and authority must be a clear, established and easy to understand by all the levels of your management.

2. Your standards and measures of performance must clearly be established.

3. The only items under this influence of your managers will be of the responsibility centers and will be included in your reports of the performance evaluation. Your managers should never be evaluated according to matters outside of their realm of control.

Your Responsibility Centers

If you are like me, when I first heard about responsibility centers I asked myself, "what is a management center and how are they classified?" I have already briefly covered the first part of the question. Although, it remains to learn how they are classified. In fact, they are sorted according to the revenue, investments and control over your costs.

➤ **Cost Center:** What do you think the cost center is responsible for? You guessed it; costs. The cost unit is a subunit of your business that will only have control over the costs. This center will not have control over your investments and revenues such as the maintenance department, the legal department, the production department and the accounting department. You will evaluate a cost center by using a variance analysis for your costs.

➢ **Revenue Center:** Just like the cost center, your revenue center will only have control over the generated revenue. They will not have any control over your costs or investments such as the marketing and sales departments. Your revenue center can be evaluated through a variance analysis for your revenues.

➢ **Profit Center:** This is a combination of the cost and revenue centers. Your profit center will have control over both your revenues and costs. This will include branches who operate in geographically different locations. Your performance of the profit center will be evaluated by measuring a segment income which is based on the controllable costs and revenues.

➢ **Investment Center:** This center will have control over the investments, costs and revenues such as its fixed assets, inventory and the receivables. Your investment center is given the authority to make decisions over your investments, which will allow it to operate as an entity that is separate such as your subsidiaries and corporate headquarters. There are profitability measures that are different that are used to evaluate your investment center. These measures include economic value-added, residual income and your return on investments.

Chapter 4 –Understanding and Managing Costs

I often come across businesses who do not understand costs. Understanding them is only half the battle. Once you understand how they work the trick is figuring out how to manage them. My goal throughout this chapter is to bring that understanding to you as the owner and manager of your business. Management accounting is great, but if you do not understand the aspects of the accounting system, it will not do you any good.

Ok, so you think you know what costs are. You are probably thinking, "I make a sale and each sale has a cost attached to it; thus the profit is the sale minus that cost." Yep, you have it all figured out. You can now put down the book and start making those sales. Oh wait, but if you want to succeed with all those sales, you may want to classify your costs. Do not forget about the overhead. Which are your variable and fixed costs? Also, have you performed a variance analysis? Now that I have your attention, how much do you really understand about costs and do you know how to manage them effectively? There's a lot more to costs than people initally think.

Classifying and the Behavior of Costs

A crucial area for managers is their understanding of the cost behaviors. In other words, this chapter is highly important for you to read and understand. In fact, do not just put the book down after you read it. Use it as a guide or reference for the future success of your business. Through a cost behavior analysis, you will study how certain costs behave in your business. You will learn how costs will change in your organization's level of activity. There are three main types of costs with which you will be working.

Fixed Costs: These costs are the ones which do not change the level of activity within a relevant range. Which means, these costs will incur even if there are no units produced such as your rent expenses, straight-line depreciation expense, etc. As there is an increase in production, your fixed cost per unit will decrease.

Variable Costs: These costs will change in a direct proportion to the level of production. Which means the total variable cost will increase when more units are produced while they will decrease when less units are produced. Even though the totals are variable, the costs are constant per units.

Mixed Costs: These costs are also known as semi-variable costs. They will have the properties of both your fixed and variable costs due to the presence of both components that is in them such as a telephone or delivery cost. Keep in mind, your phone will have a fixed cost for the phone subscription, but will have a variable cost as you typically get charged per minutes. If you do not have the minute charge and it is one price for unlimited calling, it will be considered a fixed price. With a delivery cost, you will have a fixed amount for a component of depreciation costs and a variable cost when you add in the fuel expense. You should know that mixed costs are not useful in their raw form. That means they will need to be split into their fixed and variable components through using cost behavior analysis techniques such as the High-Low Method, Scatter Diagram Method and the Regression Analysis.

We talk about different analysis that can be used in the different situations. Even though different analyses can be used with mixed costs, the most common and easiest is the high-low method. The majority of majors will use this method to classify and analyze the mixed costs into fixed or variable costs. With only the variable costs changing when the activity level changes, it allows for the high-low method to differentiate between the two different costs or levels. There are two easy steps to this method:

1. Determine your Variable Cost per Unit

2. Determine your Fixed Costs by subtracting the total variable cost at either the high or the low activity level from the total cost at the activity level.

Under the Generally Accepted Accounting Principles (GAAP) the costing behavior is not required for your external reporting. However, the understanding of cost behavior is highly important for your management to plan and control the organizational costs. The budgets and variance reports are more effective when you understand and can reflect on the patterns from cost behaviors. It is also necessary to have this understanding when you calculate your break-even point and any other type of cost-volume-profit analysis. Even though the GAAP does not require it, it is vital for you to understand it.

The cost behavior is the manner where the changes in your business activities impact expenses. That means your managers should be aware of cost behaviors when they construct the annual budget to anticipate whether any of the costs will spike or decline.

As you can see, cost behavior is essential to your business. Although, is it the only important aspect that you need to be concerned with? Of course not. You and your managers should be aware and knowledgeable of the effects of your costs on profits. The easiest way to find this information is through a cost-volume-profit analysis. This analysis will study the effects of the changes in your costs and volume within the profile of your company. It is important to your business for controlling costs and for-profit planning and budgeting. Through this analysis, you can make decisions with the selling prices, determine the product mix and maximize the use of your production facilities.

One of the most common expressions in the business world is, "profitability is just around the corner." Granted, this is the basic goal and what every business owner is trying to achieve. Do people achieve it? Perhaps! Here is the reality of it though: many businesses do not make it. Having a business is not easy. In fact, it is tough - profits are elusive and competition has a habit of moving into areas where profits are available. This is an area that will not change. The good news is that it can be overcome through management accounting and other techniques you have been learning.

There is an unlimited supply of stories of businesses who have struggled to get through the beginning stages of their business. If you follow these stories and watch them through the ups and downs, there will be one thing all the successful businesses have in common. They never gave up and through the proper analysis had gone onto great success. One company that had overcome these struggles is McDonalds.

Ask yourself; what is characteristic of your business? This is a great question as it will define your essential structure with your fixed costs. Let me give you a few different examples to illustrate this point. An airline has a big burden with their costs that are fixed. These costs are related to everything that is associated with running an airline. Remember, those costs are things such as the maintenance of the aircrafts, the ability for guests to make reservations, the individual gates at the many different airports and the aircraft. During the lean years they struggle and many times are unable to cover the fixed costs. However, during the boom years they are extremely profitable as these fixed costs will not increase with the volume. When you think about it, it does not matter if you fly the plane with no passengers vs when you fly with a full plane. The costs will remain the same. You could also look at a software company. They have investments associated with the development of their products and small costs that are involved in the process of reproducing the various electronic copies that are for the finished product, thus keeping the variable costs low.

The point is your business is distinctive. You should fully understand the structure of the costs for your business. Most business trends used to be that the fixed cost was increasing. Much of it was because of the growing investment in the robotics area and the technology area. These components will need to become affordable. There will now be some outsourcing that may eliminate a few of the benefits for your employees.

Some economists talk about the concept that focuses on the scale of the economies. Some efficiencies are achieved as you increase the level of production. You should know that this may have several forms. Your fixed costs may unfurl over a large production run and will cause a decrease with the fixed cost for each unit. What about your heightened buying power such as discounts for your quantity? As your volume goes up, it can lessen the variable costs for each unit. These are credible considerations which should be taken into examination in the business evaluation. Always remember that care must be taken to limit your analysis with an applicable range of activities. This pertinent range will be your anticipated level of activity. Any data that has your pricing outside this area is unnecessary and does not need to be considered. With your relevant range, you must also consider your evaluation of the fixed costs.

Cost Behavior Analysis

Being able to perform a cost behavior analysis is very important within management accounting. This analysis will help your management to attempt to understand how your operating costs will change in relation to a change within your organization's activity level. Typically, these costs may include materials, direct labor and your overhead costs that are incurred from the product development. This analysis will usually be performed through the mathematical cost functions. For example, your total variable costs will change in relation to the increase in activity while your fixed costs will remain the same. This means your cost functions may come in several forms.

Your cost functions can usually be plotted on a graph, and you would use the formula $y = mx + b$. For you to determine these cost functions, two assumptions can be made to simplify this analysis.

- ➢ Variations in the cost driver explain the variations in the related total costs.

- ➢ Cost behavior can be summarized into a linear cost function within a relevant range.

Your relevant range will refer to the range of your activities in which the relationship between the total cost and the level of activity that is maintained. Keep in mind: in a real-life situation, you will find that not all your cost functions are linear and will not be explained by a single cost driver.

Quantitative Cost Analysis

It is common for your management to use a quantitative analysis method to show your cost functions. The easiest of these methods will be the high-low method. Through this method, you will only use the highest and lowest values of your cost drivers and its respective costs for you to determine the cost function. As with any method there are limitations to the high-low method. This is simply a first attempt to examine the relationship between your cost driver and your overall costs.

Another method of this analysis will be the regression analysis. This is a statistical method that will measure the average amount of change in your dependent variable associated with the changes in your independent variable. This will be a much better indicator of the relationship between the variables. A great tool for this analysis and many others is Microsoft Excel.

Advantages of Classifying Cost

I am sure you are wondering why you should classify your costs? There are a few advantages to this and I want to ensure you know what they are.

Profit Planning: The primary objective of your business is to earn profits. This will make it very important to use profit planning. You will be concerned with taking a series of decisions and selecting among the various alternatives available, which will make studying the behavior or costs and profits in relation to changes in your volume output very important.

Effective Cost Control: Your profits can be increased through an effective cost control and cost reduction. Classification of your costs into fixed and variable elements will help your management control costs effectively as your fixed costs will be incurred by the decisions of management and controlled only by your top management. However, your variable costs may be controlled at the lowest levels of management.

Fixation of Selling Prices: Your profits could be maximized by either reduction and control over costs or through increasing the sales value through increase in your sales volume or price. The fixation of proper selling prices is highly important for your management. The segregation of costs into your fixed and variable elements will enable your management to adopt the most appropriate selling price policy as sometimes one may have to sell even below your total costs. Your selling prices should not be below the variable costs.

Marginal Costing and Break-Even Analysis: One basic assumption of marginal costing is the breakeven analysis, and cost-volume-profit analysis is how they are elements of costs which can be segregated into your fixed and variable costs. This makes the use of marginal costing and break-even techniques an essential part of classification of your costs.

Budgetary Control: For the preparation of flexible budgets and effective budgetary control, this classification is a pre-requisite. Your flexible budget will be designed to change in accordance with the level of your activities, and hence the cost behavior will be important.

Proper Absorption of Overheads: The analytical study of the behavior of costs will also help in proper absorption of overhead as the method is adopted for the absorption and depends on the nature of your overhead.

Helpful in Decision-Making: The classifications of your costs into fixed and variable elements will help your management in making decisions such as if they should make or buy the product, selection of a proper product mix, capacity decisions and if they should operate or close the business. These classifications are essential for the ascertainment of cost, profit planning, cost control and decision-making alike.

Allocating Overhead

You hear me talk about overhead all the time. The problem is that most of us do not know how to allocate your overhead or even know what I am talking about. In fact, you can allocate overhead cost by any reasonable measure if it is consistently applied across your reporting periods. That makes it a little easier to understand. You can do what you want with allocating overhead if you do it the same throughout your reporting periods. The common bases of allocation are your direct labor hours that are charged against a product or the number of machine hours that are used during production of that product.

Your overhead is a common expense that is incurred for several of your departments and cost centers. The process of charging items of your overhead is known as allocation of overhead. The allocation of specific overhead costs to produce goods is required under the rules of various accounting frameworks. Many businesses show the amount of overhead to be allocated as being substantially greater than the direct cost of goods. Because of this, the allocation method can be of some importance.

When you are operating your business, you will encounter one of two types of overhead. These overheads are administrative overhead and manufacturing overhead. The point is you will always have one of these types of overhead.

Administrative Overhead: These will include costs that are not involved in the development or production of goods or services such as the costs of your front office administration and sales. This type of overhead is essential and does not include the manufacturing overhead.

Manufacturing Overhead: These types of overhead will be the costs that a factory will incur other than their direct costs. You will need to allocate the costs of your manufacturing overhead to any inventory items that are classified as work-in-process or finished goods. Your overhead will not be allocated to the raw materials inventory as your operations is giving rise to overhead costs only through the impact of work-in-process and finished goods inventory. Here is a short list of items that are usually included in your manufacturing overhead:

Depreciation of factory equipment	Quality control and inspection
Factory administration expenses	Rent, facility and equipment
Indirect labor and production supervisory wages	Repair expenses
Indirect materials and supplies	Rework labor, scrap and spoilage
Maintenance, factory and production equipment	Taxes related to production assets
Officer salaries related to production	Uncapitalized tools and equipment
Production employees' benefits	Utilities

The typical procedure for allocating overhead will be to accumulate all your manufacturing overhead costs into one or two cost pools. Then you will take them and use an activity measure to apportion your overhead costs into the cost pools to inventory. You can use this formula to help with the allocation: **Overhead Allocation Per Unit = Cost Pool / Total Activity Measure**.

Essentially there two kinds of overhead costs. I want you to think about what your costs are to the project you are working on. This will help determine which overhead costs you will be using.

Indirect Costs: These costs are your expenses that are related to your job activity. They can be tied to either multiple jobs or just one job. That means if you have several projects they could be responsible for the expenses. There are several benefits to this as not all jobs within the projects will relate to the expenses equally.

General and Administrative (G&A) Costs: These costs might be one that is applied to the general running of your business. All the projects will probably benefit equally. For example, you will have office rent and utilities, administrative salaries, advertising, general liability insurance to just name a few. G&A supports your ability to take new jobs and bill them accordingly. They are relatively stable despite fluctuation in your job progress and labor.

There are many options in the allocation of overhead where the first rule is to know what you do not know. It really comes down to research and finding the answers to the unknown. To get you started, I want you to think about what the costs are, what methods to use and what technology you have. This is a great place to begin, and then you can consider the following three basic steps to use job costing successfully.

Gather Your Costs: During our first step, you must know what your costs are. Start by asking yourself, "What are my real costs of completing this job?" This is where it becomes helpful to think through your overhead and G&A types of indirect costs.

Select Your Method: Selecting a method for allocating overhead is important. This method can vary depending on the needs of your business.

- ➤ **Establishing a Basis:** Part of defining what cost pools you may want to allocate to your jobs is also figuring out how you want to distribute them. We can look at total direct costs, direct labor costs, direct labor hours and equipment cost as only a few options a contractor may use for allocating overhead. Selecting a basis for allocating indirect costs should make sense for the type of cost and for your type of business.

It is also important to figure out how you are going to allocate your costs.

- ➤ **Using a Predetermined Rate:** For example, contractors can choose to estimate their overhead for each job using an established rate. You may calculate your overhead for a job through a general representation of x% of revenue or y% of its direct labor costs. When you allocate your overhead, you will add that amount to your total costs. This is the simplest method, but it is less accurate.

- ➤ **Using a Proportion Among Jobs:** Contractors usually have multiple jobs and can track each overhead cost in their G/L and proportionally distribute them across all the jobs.

Get the Technology You Need: Having the right tools for the job is hugely important. Technology has come so far that the hardest jobs are now much more manageable. Depending on the size of your business, spreadsheets simply may not be a realistic, long-term option for tracking and managing your overhead allocation. However, there is some excellent general-purpose accounting software that can work very well for small contractors.

Job Costing

Job costing is also known as job order costing. Therefore, if you ever hear the term of job order costing, they are talking about the same thing. This type of costing is best suited for those type of situations where the goods and services are produced upon receipt of a customer order, according to customer specifications or in a separate batch. For example, we can follow a shipbuilder. They would likely accumulate costs for each ship produced. This is only one example as each job is unique.

I want to take you on a journey into the land of job costing as we follow an example company through the process.

Anthony Vandyke owns an electrical contracting company, Vandyke Electric. Anthony provides a variety of products and services to his clientele. He has four employees, a rented shop, a broad inventory of parts and a fleet of five service trucks. On a typical day, Anthony will arrive at the shop early and line out the day's work assignments. Around 8:00 a.m., his electricians arrive and he gives them each their assignments. They are also given the necessary parts and the equipment they will need for each job. Anthony then dispatched them to their various jobs.

Throughout the rest of this example, I am going to follow Tony, who is one of Anthony's electricians. I will then show you at the end how everything comes together with all the technicians as they will follow the same procedures for each of their jobs as Tony will be doing for his.

On May 30, Tony arrived at the shop at 8:00 a.m. He first spent 30 minutes getting his assignments and loading a service truck with the necessary items to complete the day's work. His three tasks for the day are as follows:

> **Job A:** Cleaning and Reconnecting the electrical connections and replacing a flood light atop a billboard (materials required include one lamp at $150).

> **Job B:** Replacing the breakers on an old electrical distribution panel at an office building (materials required include 20 breakers at $20 each making it $400 total).

> ➢ **Job C:** Pulling wire for a new residence that is under construction (materials required include 500 feet of wire at $0.14 per foot making it $70 total).

Tony completed all three tasks. He spent one hour on the billboard, two hours on the electrical panel and three hours on the residential installation. The other two hours of his 8-hour day were spent on indirect job administration and travel. Throughout the day, Tony also used a roll of electrical tape ($3) and a box of wire nuts (60 nuts at $0.05 each making it $3 total). Donnie is paid $18 per hour. He drove a truck and used a variety of tools, ladders and other specialized equipment. Anthony is paid $25 per hour and does not work on any specific jobs. Instead, his time is spent doing inspections, getting permits, managing inventory and other tasks.

Ask yourself, "How much did it cost to complete each job?" Naturally, each job has the direct costs of the job such as the materials needed and Tony's labor time to complete the task. Keep in mind: none of the jobs could have been completed without the shop, equipment, trucks, indirect labor time, tape, wire nuts and so forth. This equipment will be considered indirect costs, or overhead. How are these costs assigned to a specific job? Now if you can answer this question without looking ahead then my job is done and you can put this book down. However, I encourage you to keep reading as I will continue this journey not by just explaining it to you through words. You will see first-hand the recording process and get a very clear picture of how job costing works.

Tracking Labor: A good relevant point to start from will be tracking labor costs. This is probably the easiest so let's get started with that first. Tony and all his associates will fill out their time report and document the time they spend each day and will also include the time spent on other tasks.

VanDyke Electric Employee: Tony Date: 5/30/2018					Daily Time Sheet	
Start Time	Stop Time	Job Name	Task	Client	Admin Hours	Direct Labor Hours
8:00	8:30	Admin	Assignment and load	n/a	0.50	
8:30	8:45	Travel		n/a	0.25	
8:45	9:45	Job A	Service and replace bulb	Image Advertising		1.00
9:45	10:15	Travel		n/a	0.50	
10:15	12:15	Job B	Replace breakers	TechWay Office Park		2.00
12:15	1:00	Lunch	n/a	n/a		
1:00	4:00	Job C	Pull wiring	Lybrand Home		0.13
4:00	4:45	Travel and Admin	Return to shop and unload	n/a	0.75	
					2.00	3.13

Tracking Material: As an electrician, it is important to keep track of your own jobs to submit to the business. The same goes for the materials used so the inventory can be updated. Tony keeps a detailed record of the materials that were released to him for each task. When Peter gathered each item for the jobs, some of them were placed in a "check out" status. That means he needs to keep track of how much is used so the remainder of the materials can be "checked in." This document is called a "materials requisition form." By using this form, it is easy to document the inventory.

VanDyke Electric Employee: Tony Date: 5/30/2018				Materials Requisition
Material	Job Name	Quantity	Per Unit Cost	Extended Cost
Light Bulbs	Job A	1 Unit	150.00	150.00
Breakers	Job B	20 Units	$20 each	400.00
Wire	Job C	500 Feet	$0.14 Per Foot	70.00
Electrical Tape	Indirect Material	1 Roll	$3 Per Roll	3.00
Wire Nuts	Indirect Material	60 Nuts	$0.05 each	3.00

Tracking Overhead: Peter would experience a massive struggle if he were to trace all the items of overhead by hand. Tracking your overhead can be a little precarious. This can be done in several different ways; however, this is one of the ways that makes it a little easier for predetermining the overhead rate. Let's assume that Peter considered all his overhead in production that could be anticipated throughout the year such as Tony's time, insurance, vehicle cost, rent, utilities, materials that are indirect and labor that is indirect. This is just to name a few.

Based on all these costs we have $150,000 as a total cost. Peter anticipates his electricians will have a total of 7,500 for the direct labor hours throughout the year. When we compare these numbers of $150,000 with 7,500 hours, there could be a possibility it will show the direct overhead as $20 for each direct labor hour. Peter has now determined a logical rate for the overhead application.

There are two areas I want to bring to your attention to regarding overhead. The first is how an overhead application will be frivolous. Peter elected to spread the overhead situated on the direct labor hours; of course, this will be the common choice; however, it is not the exclusive choice. The second area is to expect inequality between actual overhead with the amount that will be applied to the production. Peter will likely determine that actual overhead will be about $150,000. He will find his electricians working about 7,500 hours that is anticipated.

Job Cost Sheet: Earlier we were tracking labor which did include some of the job information. Now Tony has a Job Costing Sheet for each job. This starts to break down the costs for each job. One thing I want you to note is the source document. Look at source document DTS.05.14.18.DO. This also shows the daily time sheet for Tony on May 30, 2018. Each source document number will be in this fashion. The overhead was applied directly to the job cost sheets based upon the predetermined overhead application scheme of $20 per direct labor hour.

VanDyke Electric Job:	Job A - Image Advertising											Job Cost Sheet
		Direct Labor			Direct Material			Applied Overhead				
	Form Reference	Hours	Rate	Total	Qty.	Unit Cost	Total	Basis	Qty.	Rate	Total	Total
30-May-18												
Tony	DTS.05.30.18.DO	1.00	$18	$18.00								$ 18.00
Light Bulb	MR.05.30.18.DO				1.00	$150	$150.00					$150.00
Applied Overhead								Labor Hours	1.00	$20	$20.00	$ 20.00
		1.00		$18.00			$150.00				$20.00	$188.00

| VanDyke Electric | | Direct Labor | | | Direct Material | | | Applied Overhead | | | | Job Cost Sheet |
| Job: Job C - Lybrand Home | | | | | | | | | | | | |
	Form Reference	Hours	Rate	Total	Qty.	Unit Cost	Total	Basis	Qty.	Rate	Total	Total
30-maj-18												
Tony	DTS.05.30.18.DO	3,00	$ 18	$ 54,00								$ 54,00
Wire	MR.05.30.18.DO				500	$ 0,04	$ 70,00					$ 70,00
Applied Overhead								Labor Hours	3,00	$ 20	$60,00	$ 60,00
		3,00		$ 54,00			$ 70,00				$60,00	$ 184,00

| VanDyke Electric | | Direct Labor | | | Direct Material | | | Applied Overhead | | | | Job Cost Sheet |
| Job: Job B - TechWay Office Park | | | | | | | | | | | | |
	Form Reference	Hours	Rate	Total	Qty.	Unit Cost	Total	Basis	Qty.	Rate	Total	Total
30-May-18												
Tony	DTS.05.30.18.DO	2.00	$18	$ 36.00								$ 36.00
Breakers	MR.05.30.18.DO				20	$ 20	$ 400.00					$ 400.00
Applied Overhead								Labor Hours	2.00	$ 20	$40.00	$ 40.00
		2.00		$ 36.00			$ 400.00				$40.00	$ 476.00

This has been a pretty basic example of job costing. However, it does not consider the sophistication of an information system that are used to track job costs. It also does not show the debits and credits that are needed to track the accumulation and application of costs within your companies' general ledger.

Process Costing

When you are working with management accounting, sometimes you will hear about process accounting. This term is usually used within the realm of cost accounting. This is one method that is used for collecting and assigning manufacturing costs to the units that are produced. When almost identical units are produced in mass production you would use process costing.

Remember, process costing is an accounting methodology that traces and accumulates direct costs and will allocate the indirect costs of a manufacturing process. You will normally see this type of cost used in industries like a bakery, toy manufacturing and so on.

I am sure you are wondering if this is the same as job costing. There is a difference. Process costing is on the terms of mass production such as a manufacturer. You saw an example of job costing earlier. Basically, job costing is on an individual basis. That means the thing to remember is the size you will be working with. Whenever you have a production process that contains some mass manufacturing and some customized elements, then you will use a hybrid costing system. In many industries, process costing is the only reasonable approach for determining product costs.

There are three types of process costing methods that are used. As we go through each of these, it is important to note that the last in, first out (LIFO) method is not one of the methods used in process costing.

The Weighted Average Costs: This method will assume that all your costs, whether from a preceding period or the current one, will be lumped together and assigned to your units that are produced. This is the easiest method to calculate.

Standard Costs: This method will be based on the standard costs. Its calculations are similar to the weighted average costing, but instead the standard costs are assigned to the produced unites rather than the actual costs. Once the total costs are accumulated based on the standard costs, these totals are compared to the actual accumulated costs, making the difference to be charged to a variance account.

First-In, First-Out Costing (FIFO): This method is a more complex calculation that will create layers of costs, which means you will have a layer for each unit of production that was started in the previous production period but was not completed with another layer for any productions that were started in the current period.

The typical manner of costs flow in your process costs are how the direct material costs are added at the beginning of the process, while all other costs are generally added over the course of the production process. This is for both the direct labor and overhead. Keep in mind: your process costing system will accumulate costs when many identical units are being produced. This system then assigns the costs at the end of the accounting period. I want to simplify this a bit for you. The process in the simplest form is the following:

Direct Materials: By using either a periodic or perpetual inventory system, we can determine the amount of materials that were used during the period. We can then calculate the number of units that have begun and completed during the period to include the number of units that have begun and are not yet completed such as the work-in-progress units. Generally, we assume that the materials are added at the beginning of the production process. That means your work-in-progress units are the same as those units that are completed when you are looking from the perspective of assigning material costs. We can now assign the amount of direct materials used based on the total of fully and partially produced units.

Direct Labor: Your labor will accumulate by the units throughout the production process. Which means it is more difficult to account for than the direct materials. We can estimate the average level of completion of all the work-in-process units. Then we can assign a standard direct labor cost based on the percentage. We can also assign the full standard labor cost to all the units that began and were completed in the period.

Overhead: Your overhead will be assigned in a manner that is like the direct labor, where we estimate the average level of completion of all the work-in-progress units and then assign the standard amount of overhead based on that percentage. We can then assign the full standard amount of overhead to all the units that began and were completed in the period.

The cost that is assigned to the units produced or are work-in-process will be recorded in the inventory asset account where it will be able to appear in the balance sheet. Eventually, when goods are sold the costs will transfer to the cost of goods sold account where it will then appear on the income statement.

Your company's cost accounting system may not mix well with the process costing system. If this is the case, there are two other options that you can use.

The Job Costing System: This system is designed to accumulate costs for either your individual units or for small batches of production.

Hybrid Costing System: This system is where your process costing is used part of the time and job costing can be used the rest of the time. This will work better in a production environment where some of the manufacturing is through large batches and there are additional work steps that involve labor that is unique for each individual unit.

5 Steps to Process Costing: There are five steps that are in the process costing method or system.

1. **Analyze Inventory Flow:** You should start by analyzing the cost-flow model of the relevant inventory account to determine how much inventory was at the beginning of the period, how much was started during the period, how much was completed during the period and how much is still left as work-in-process at the end of the period.

2. **Convert In-Process Inventory to Equivalent Units:** Next you need to convert your work-in-process ending inventory into many equivalent units that are produced. For example, if you have 1,000 units of inventory that are work-in-process and these units are 50% complete, then you will consider this as the equivalent of 500 units that are produced. You will calculate this as: *500 (Units Produced) = 0.50 (50% Complete) x 1,000 (Work-In-Process).*

3. **Compute All Applicable Costs:** You will now compute the totals of your direct and indirect costs that were incurred through the production process that is needing to be assigned to the units completed and the units that are still in process. This will include the costs associated with the beginning inventory and the costs that are incurred during the relevant period.

4. **Calculate the Cost Per Unit of Finished and In-Process Inventory:** You will now calculate the amount of your cost that is to be assigned to the completed units of your output and the equivalent of the completed units of your output that are still in the ending inventory. For example, if you have 2,000 units that were completed and 1,000 units were left half-finished, you will then divide the applicable costs by 2,500 units.

5. **Allocate Costs to Units of Finished and In-Process Inventory:** Finally, you will allocate your relevant costs to the units of the product that were completed and to your units of the product that are remaining in the work-in-process account.

Process Costing vs. Job Costing

Many of you are probably looking at process costing and job costing and wondering what the difference is, as they seem to be alike. In a way they are similar. However, there are a few differences between the two. Knowing these differences will help you to determine which method to use for your business.

➢ **Size of Job:** Process costing is more suited for large-scale production; whereas, job costing is more suited for tracking small production that has fewer costs. For example, if you are a big manufacturer that sell goods to businesses such as Walmart, Amazon, big lots, etc. then you will use the process costing system. However, if you are a freelancer and move from one job to the next, then you will use the job costing system as each job or product is individual and not mass produced on a large scale.

➢ **Type of Product:** Process costing will be used for standardized, mass-produced products; whereas, job costing will usually be used for custom or unique products. For example, a car manufacturer will create thousands of cars that are the same model, and thus they will use the process costing method. However, a freelance writer will produce books customized and based on the needs of each individual client which will make each book unique.

➢ **Billing Customers:** With job costing, you can customize each customer bill based on your hourly rate, cost of materials, etc.; whereas, process costing is less straightforward as the costs are aggregated.

➢ **Record Keeping:** Process costing will combine the costs and requires less to record; whereas, through job costing you will record labor, materials and overhead to the specific jobs, batches or units. These transactions will each affect a different account. For example, when you are a manufacturer and need to record the transaction all your costs for each unit will be recorded in one transaction. However, if you are a freelance writer, you will have an individual account for each area of the process such as if you bind the book yourself or send it out for it to be published this could affect two different accounts depending on what decision you are using for your business. If you send it to be published for the client, you will have a publishing type of account. If you bind the books yourself, you will have the cost of materials and equipment. This is only one thing that will come into play for a freelancer. You will also need to consider the cost of your time or labor among many other factors. If it is a fixed price for the job, the transaction is a little easier. However, you still need to do the calculations to figure out how much that fixed price will be.

Variance Analysis

Start asking yourself, "what is a Variance Analysis?" Maybe you are already asking that question. So, what about, "what is Variance?" It is hard to know what the analysis is when you may not know what variance is. In accounting, a variance is the variation between the expected or planned amount and an actual amount. For example, a variance can occur for items that are contained in a department's expense report. That means, a variance analysis is the attempts to identify and explain the reasons for the variation between a budgeted amount and the actual amount. Typically, you will see this analysis associated with a manufacturer's product costs.

When you think about it, the variances will give a snapshot of the long-term performance for a reporting period. This could indicate under or over performance during this period. Every item from your business will assess its favorability by comparing the actual costs with the standard costs for your industry. These variances can be calculated for the quantity and price of your materials, variable and labor overhead and then reported to your management. Keep in mind, not all the variances are crucial. Your management only needs to focus on the ones that are unusual or are particularly significant. Many problems can be identified through these analyses and onced fixed, the overall performance of your company will improve.

Variance Types

You will have variances for labor, materials and overhead that will consist of the quantity or efficiency. However, your fixed overhead will have a budget and volume variance. In this chart, you will see a good road map into the different variances with which you may be working.

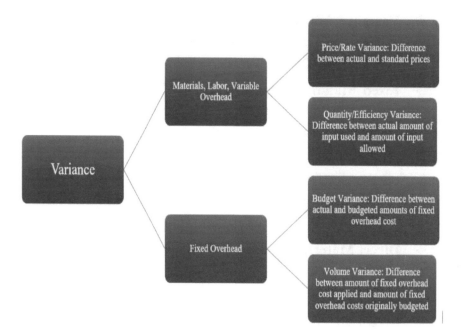

When you are calculating your variances, the easiest will be a column method where you can then record all the information. I found that it is easiest to create a spreadsheet that has each area labeled so that you only need to input the data in the right spot. Granted, creating spreadsheets can be time-consuming. Keep in mind: you only need to do this one time, and it will save a lot of time overall with the calculations.

Let's follow the following example and see how these calculations will work for each variance analysis. The scenario is really to give you information about the company and where I get the numbers for the analysis.

Your business produces several gadgets. The overhead will be applied to your products based on labor hours that will be direct hours. Your denominator will be set at 4,030 hours. Your cost card for standard costs will show the following data:

> **Direct Materials:** You will have 6 pieces for each gadget that will be at a cost of $0.50 for each piece.

> **Direct Labor:** There will be 1.3 hours associated with each gadget at a cost of $8 for each hour worked on the gadget.

> **Variable Manufacturing Overhead:** There will be 1.3 hours associated with each gadget at a cost of $4 for each hour worked on the gadget.

> **Fixed Manufacturing Overhead:** There will be 1.3 hours associated with each gadget at a cost of $6 for each hour worked on the gadget.

In January, your company had produced about 3,000 gadgets. This made your budget for your expense in fixed overhead at $24,180. Which means, the actual cost for each are on the cost card are as follows:

> **Direct Materials:** There will be 25,000 pieces that were each purchased at $0.48 per piece.

> **Direct Labor:** There will be 4,000 hours that were put into the gadget at the cost of $36,000.

> **Variable Manufacturing Overhead:** Your Actual cost will be $17,000.

> **Fixed Manufacturing Overhead:** Your Actual cost will be $25,000.

Now that we have the information for your company it is time to start performing each variance analysis.

Materials Variance: For the variance in materials we will look at the Quantity and the Price.

> For your price variance, you will multiply the Actual Quantity (AQ) with the Actual Price (AP). Then you will multiply the Actual Quantity (AQ) with the Standard Price (SP). Once you have these totals, you will then take the total from the AQ and AP and then subtract the total from the AQ and the SP. This will give you the Price Variance.

  o **AQ * AP:** 25,000 pieces * $0.48 per piece = $12,000

  o **AQ * SP:** 25,000 pieces * $0.50 = $12,500

- Price Variance: 12,500 (AQ*SP) – 12,000 (AQ*AP) = $500 (Favorable)

➢ For you to figure out the variance for the quantity, you will still need to multiply your Standard Quantity (SQ) by the Standard Price (SP). Then you will take the AQ and SP calculation and subtract the SQ and SP calculation to find your Quantity Variance.

- **SQ * SP:** 18,000 pieces * $0.50 = $9,000

- **Quantity Variance:** $9,000 (SQ*SP) - $12,500 (AQ*SP) = -$3,500 (Unfavorable)

➢ To find the variance for your materials you will subtract your Quantity Variance (QV) from your Price Variance (PV).

- **Materials Variance:** $500 (PV) - $3,500 (QV) = -$3,000 (Unfavorable)

As you can see, the materials variance is unfavorable by $3,000. This will allow for your management to look for solutions and seek a way to improve the materials variance. Keep in mind; you noticed that the price variance was found favorable. Which means the real question is, "why does your company need more materials when the standard 18,000 pieces was budgeted for?" It might be because your business received some defective materials. You may have also had a few problems and malfunctions with the machinery. However, it does give you a direction to look for the answers.

Labor Variance: Next we will look at the labor variance by calculating the hours and rate.

➢ For you to find the Rate Variance, you will need to multiply your Actual Hours (AH) by your Actual Rate (AR). Then you will need to multiply your Actual Hours (AH) by your Standard Rate (SR). Once you have these totals, you will subtract the AH and SR calculation from your AH and AR calculation.

- AH * AR: 4,000 hours * $9 = $36,000

- AH * SR: 4,000 hours * $8 = $32,000

- **Rate Variance:** 32,000 (AH*SR) - 36,000 (AH*AR) = -$4,000 (Unfavorable)

➤ For you to find the variance for efficiency, you will need to calculate your Standard Hours Allowed (SHA) by your Standard Price (SP). You will then take you're your SHA and SP calculation then subtract it from the AH and SR calculation.

- **SHA * SP:** 3,900 * $8 = $31,200

- **Efficiency Variance:** $31,200 (SHA*SP) – $32,000 (AH*SR) = -$800 (Unfavorable)

➤ For use to find the labor variance we need to take the Efficiency Variance (EV) and subtract it from the Rate Variance (RV).

- **Labor Variance:** -$4,000 (RV) – $800 (EV) = - $4,800 (Unfavorable)

Through our calculations, we can see that there is a huge issue with the overall variance being -$4,800 (Unfavorable). This is one your management needs to look at. They need to address the following question; why do we have a price for the actual labor that is higher when the standard cost would have been sufficient? They will also need to look at why there is 1,000 hours more associated with production. You can also use this example when calculating overhead costs as the variable for your overhead will be tested based on your labor hours in the example.

Fixed Overhead Variance: Your fixed overhead will be important to your business and you will need to examine your fixed overhead costs and use a few of the other areas that are used in the other variances we had just calculated.

- ➤ For us to find your budget variance, we need to find some different information. Locate your Actual Fixed Overhead Cost (AFOC) and add it to your spreadsheet. The next calculation we need will be the Budget Fixed Overhead Cost (BFOC). To find this, you will multiply your Denominator Level of Activity (DLA) by the Standard Rate (SR).

  - **BFOC:** 4,030 hours (DLA) * $6 (SR) = $24,180 (BFOC)

  - **Budget Variance:** $24,180 (BFOC) – $25,000 (AFOC) = -$820 (Unfavorable)

- ➤ Now we need to find the variance for your volume. To do this, you will find your Fixed Overhead Cost Applied to Inventory (FOCAI). To do this, you will multiply your Standard Hours Allowed (SHA) by your Standard Rate (SR).

  - **FOCAI:** 3,900 hours (SHA) * $6 (SR) = $23,400 (FOCAI)

  - **Volume Variance:** $23,400 (FOCAI) – $24,180 (BFOC) = -$780 (Unfavorable)

- ➤ You will now need to find the Fixed Overhead Variance. To do this you will subtract the Volume Variance (VV) from the Budget Variance (BV).

  - **Fixed Overhead Variance:** -$780 (VV) – $820 (BV) = -$1,600 (Unfavorable)

Yet again, you can see that your Fixed Overhead Variance is unfavorable by -$1,600. This will need to be another area for your management to address.

A simple company that you thought was doing well by looking at the numbers has a completely different story once the variance analysis is performed. Granted you may be doing well; however, we now see the areas that will allow for your business to do even better.

Chapter 5 – Budgeting Like a Pro

It does not matter how big or small your business is. Your budget is essential and must be done. In fact, while you read this chapter, I want you to pull out and look at your own business budget. What do you see? Are you still within budget? Do you need to redo your budget? These are basic questions you should be asking every month. Do not create a budget because you needed it for your business plan and then never look at it again.

We are now going to shift gears slightly and look at your capital budget. This type of budget is sometimes considered an investment appraisal. This is due to how it will help your business determine whether projects may be worth pursuing. A good rule to follow is if the project or investment will increase the value of your company. For example, investing in a new coffee maker will not increase value or make you money. However, investing in repairs for a piece of equipment that is used to bring profit to your business would be a good investment. That means, do not let it collect dust in the filing cabinet. Pull it out and start using it for what it was meant to be used for.

The purpose of your capital budget is for planning. In fact, when used correctly it will be the most powerful planning tool you have for success. This budget will help you to create accountability and measurability. To give you an idea of the importance, there are several techniques I want you to consider. These techniques can be used by your management while utilizing your capital budget.

➤ Payback Period

➤ Discounted Payback Period

➤ Net Present Value

➤ Accounting Rate of Return

➤ Internal Rate of Return

➤ Profitability Index

To make it simple, this process is used for determining and evaluating your probable expenses and investments that can be huge for your business. Many times, a proposed project's lifetime has cash outflows and inflows that will be examined to decide if the projected returns that will be generated will meet an acceptable target gauge.

There are different methods of your capital budgeting that can be used. Out of all these methods, three are the most popular when choosing the best projects. You should obtain your investment funds before the other projects. The three methods are the Payback period analysis, DCF analysis and the throughput analysis.

Throughput Analysis: This analysis will show the material that passes through the system. This will be a complicated form of your capital budgeting analysis; however, it will be the best for being accurate as it helps your management decide which project are worth pursuing. Through this method, it considers your entire business as a single system that generates profit.

With this analysis, it speculates that most costs within this system will be considered expenses from the operations. Which means your business will need to maximize its throughput for your whole system to pay your expenses to maximize your profits that will expand the throughput which will pass through the bottleneck of the operation. This bottleneck refers to the resources in your system which will require the lengthiest time during your operations. Which means, your management team will always give high consideration to your capital budget projects which will increase and impact the throughput as it passes through the bottleneck.

DCF Analysis: This analysis will be like the NPV analysis as it will look at its beginning cash outflow that is needed for funding a project, cash mix of the inflows from its form of your revenue and any future outflows that are in the form of the maintenance to include any other types of costs. The results from your DCF analysis will be the NPV. The projects that have the highest in NPV will rank supreme to any of the other projects except if one or more will be exclusive.

Payback Analysis: This method is the easiest type of the capital budgeting and is also the least accurate. So why use it, you wonder. That is easy: As you run a business, there is not always time to perform the other analysis and you need something fast. It is a method that will give your managers a perceptive of the effectiveness of the projects or group of projects. It will simply give you an idea of the length of time it takes for your company to regain its investments from your project.

The Basics of Management Budgeting

Whoever said being a manager is easy may need to see a doctor. The fact is, it is all about planning. Granted, to some planning may be easy. However, think of all the factors you have been faced with while running and operating your business. Budgets should be your managers best friends. Maybe even consider taking them out to lunch. You laugh but how many times do you find yourself thinking about going over your budget at work and never do? Take your planning tools to lunch with your management team and discuss it over a nice meal. You will be amazed at what you can accomplish through this technique. Your budgets are the main tool your managers will have for planning and having financial control in the business. It does not need to be fancy. It is simply a written statement of the manager's plans for a period in financial terms.

Why Create a Budget: Creating a budget will bring you some great benefits to your company that will push your business into future success.

- ➢ Require management to plan ahead
- ➢ Give definite objectives for all levels in your company
- ➢ Create an early warning system to prevent potential problems
- ➢ Facilitate the coordination of activities
- ➢ Helps your managers stay aware of financial transactions
- ➢ Can help to motivate your employees

Your budgets can be created for any period. I think about them like goals. You should create a budget for the entire year. Maybe you will want to extend that goal. Create a five-year budget. Outline everything that you think may come up within five years. Once this is done, create a 1-year goal to help you monitor your progress to achieve the long-term budget or goal. Then you can break it down to six months and then finally a monthly budget. With you knowing your 5-year and 1-year budgets you can modify your monthly budgets to keep you on track for the future goals. Do not take this lightly. This is your business and your future. It takes time and hard work to manage your budget and stay on track.

You want to see a successful future. When you are creating your budgets, regardless of how far out they are, you should remember these principles:

- ➢ Your budget should have a sound organizational structure
- ➢ It requires effective research and analysis
- ➢ All levels of your management must also accept it

Once your budget has passed through these areas and is now in effect, it should be used to evaluate your employees and managers performances. As it is used as a planning tool, dig out the old budgets and accounting data to ensure you are on the up throughout your business and on track to meet or exceed your goals.

This is only one picture of the pie. It does not show everything there is to know about what your business is doing financially. You will find that there are multiple budgets that show different financial areas within your business. This is where you will have a master budget that shows everything that is contained in all the different budgets. This budget will contain your operating budgets and your financial budgets.

Master Budget: The budget is considered your master blueprint for the entire company. It will detail the financials for every department and every budget. Based off of this budget, several sub-budgets are created, such as a separate budget for operations, external financing, capital improvements and support services. Each of these budgets will contain information that is related to a specific financial goal for your company. After each budget is created, your accountant will combine them all into one large master budget for an executive review. The process for creating the master budget is a time consuming lengthy process and is usually done on an annual basis.

Operating Budget: This budget is a sub-budget with a kick. It is highly important as it has all the information that is related to sales and income for the coming fiscal period. Usually, this budget is created annually; however, it is the main operating budget and may include several monthly budgets throughout the year. You will include information such as sales forecasts, manufacturing costs, inventory and operating expenses. Each of these areas will combine to make up the necessary financial outlays that are needed to generate sales for your business.

Financial Budget: This budget will include the capital expenditures, cash budgets and your budgeting balance sheet. This information could have valuable information for where your finances are standing. As you can see it also consists of smaller budgets that may be departmental type budgets.

Flexible Budget: This budget is important as they are used by manufacturing and service companies to measure the production costs of goods and services. These budgets are an active part of the daily operations as it tracks the cost variances from the production process.

Contribution Margin

It seems like if you run a business, knowing how profitable your business is comes naturally. "I can feel it if there is something wrong." However, we also know it takes much more than a feeling to have a prosperous future for your business. It is essential to understand how profitable your business can be. Most of you will probably look at the profit margin. This is a great place to start as it does measure the total amount by which revenue from sales will exceed the costs. However, if you really want to understand how a specific product contributes to your business profit, you must look at the contribution margin.

The contribution margin is another way to look at your profits. Sit back and think about how your company's income statement typically works. You will start with the revenue and subtract your cost of goods sold (COGS) to get your gross profit. You then subtract the operating expenses to get the operating profit. Now you will subtract the taxes, interests and everything else to net your net profit. Now let's simplify this by taking out all the variables and this will get you the contribution margin. Now we have a calculation that looks like this: *contribution margin = revenue – variable costs.*

A great place to start is using your traditional income statement and recategorizing all the costs as fixed or variable. This is not a straightforward process even though it may sound like it. These fixed and variable costs are not always clear which category they would fall into. Remember, your fixed costs are business costs that remain the same no matter how many of your products or services you produce.

Pricing

The costs of your products in managerial accounting will be those costs which are crucial to manufacturing a product. Your product costs will be equivalent to the value of your direct material and labor costs, and the costs of your manufacturing overhead. The actual costing method will be able to determine your costs for your overall products and the costs of your products for each unit which is based on the actual cost that you acquired during that period.

Direct Materials: These will be materials that your business will use for the manufacturing of products that can be traced straight to the products like a bicycle tire that is on the exact bicycle. You will want to calculate the costs from the direct materials that you will use over a period, like one month, that will determine the total direct materials costs.

Direct Labor: These are the costs that you will obtain to engage your workers that will assemble and manufacture the products directly. The costs will include taxes, your payroll, life contributions, wages, etc. You will add these costs that you incurred for the month to determine the total costs from your direct labor.

Manufacturing Overhead: These costs are necessary to make your product; however, it cannot be traced to any product specifically. These costs may include your indirect materials like the masking tape and your costs from indirect labor like your costs from employing a skillful maintenance worker. You may also have in these costs the utilities, taxes from your property and rent. You will add the costs from your manufacturing overhead that you obtained throughout the month that will determine your total costs from your manufacturing costs.

Product Cost and Product Cost Per Unit: You will take the total costs from the direct materials, total costs from the direct labor and the total costs from the manufacturing overhead and add them all together. This will regulate the total costs of your products. Now you will take the total product costs and divide it by the total products you had manufactured throughout the period and this will determine your costs for each unit.

You can use pricing strategies to seek various types of the objectives like the expansion of your profit shares, increasing your market shares and pushing out your competitors from the market. As the market is consistently changing it can be important for your company to modify your pricing strategies. Several pricing strategies could be used. I am going to give you a handful that will get you started in the right direction.

Cost-Based Pricing Strategies: These will be the strategies that are established through the costs of your underlying services or products, such as:

- ➤ **Absorption Pricing:** These include the costs that are variable to include the allocation of your fixed costs. They could or could not include the markup from profits.

- ➤ **Break-Even Pricing:** These will be the setting from the exact point of a price which your business will earn no profit due to an examination of your variable costs which include the estimate of each unit sold.

- ➤ **Cost Plus Pricing:** These will include the fixed costs that are allocated, a markup percentage that has been predetermined and the variable costs.

- ➤ **Marginal Cost Pricing:** These are the prices which have been set close to your marginal costs that will be required for producing an item which will usually take advantage of the production capacity that is otherwise unused.

- ➤ **Time and Materials Pricing:** With this pricing, you will bill your customers for the materials and labor that are acquired by your business with a markup in profit.

Value Pricing Strategies: These types of strategies will not build upon the costs. Instead, they rely on the opinion of your customers point of view will add value to your services and products such as:

➢ **Dynamic Pricing:** This is technology that will be used for altering prices continuously based on the customer's willingness to pay.

➢ **Premium Pricing:** This is the method of price setting that sets prices greater than the rate of the market to give the product or service an exclusivity aura.

➢ **Price Skimming:** This is the system for first placing the prices high to gain high profits that are unusual as the product was first introduced.

➢ **Value Pricing:** These prices will be set established through the anticipated value of your services and products to your customers.

Teaser Pricing Strategies: These are types of strategies that are established from a concept of luring your customers through some free products or lower-priced items, then cross-sell the products with high-priced products. Examples include:

➢ **Freemium Pricing:** This is the method that offers a service that is basically free and then charges more of a price for a better level of service.

➢ **High-Low Pricing:** This is the method for pricing some products at or below the rate of the market to entice customers to come in and then price all the rest of the items higher than the rate of the market.

➢ **Loss Leader Pricing:** This is the method for offering a special deal for a few items hoping to draw in customers who will buy other items that are regularly-priced.

Strategic Pricing Strategies: These types of strategies involves using the pricing of the product to position your business within the market or leave out the competitors completely such as:

➢ **Limit Pricing:** This is the method for setting a very low and long-term price which will avert your potential competitors so they will not want to enter the market.

➢ **Penetration Pricing:** This is the method for setting the price under the rate of the market so you can increase the shares within the market.

➢ **Predatory Pricing:** This is the method for marking the prices low enough so it will push the competition out of the market.

➢ **Price Leadership:** This is when one business will set the price point and your competitors accept it.

Miscellaneous Pricing Strategies: These types of strategies will be separate concepts that are not going to be related with the previous categories.

➢ **Psychological Pricing:** This is the method for price setting that will set the price slightly lower from the rounded price with the assumption that your customers may consider your prices to be much lower than they are.

➢ **Shadow Pricing:** This is the position of your product as an item that is intangible which does not have a market price.

➢ **Transfer Pricing:** This is the price where your product will be sold through one subsidiary of your main business to another.

Chapter 6 – Forecasting Tools for Business Trends

Any good company knows how important it is to follow the trends of business. Forecasting is one of those areas that you need many tools at your disposal. There are so many tools that it is hard to cover them all.

A good place to start is with the ratios you could use. These calculations are used to determine many things about how your company is doing, how the market is doing and how your company compares to the market. Keep in mind: anyone who has some type of interest in your company will be using these ratios to determine how your company is doing or will do in the future. There are a few basic ratios I want you to remember.

The key ratios I want you to remember are:

- ➢ **Current Ratio:** Current Ratio = Current Assets / Current Liabilities

- ➢ **Return on Equity (ROE):** ROE = Net Income / Average Stockholders' Equity

- ➢ **Debt-Equity (D/E) Ratio:** D/E = Total Liabilities / Total Stockholders' Equity

- ➢ **Dividend Payout Ratio:** Dividend Payout Ratio = Cash Dividends / Net Income

> **Price/Earnings (P/E) Ratio:** P/E = Market Price of Common Stock Per Share / Earnings Per Share

I wanted to point out these key ratios as they are the easiest to calculate and will give you all the information you need to help run your business. Several different ratios are also split up into six categories.

1. **Liquidity Ratios:** These will measure your company's ability to pay off your short-term debts as they come due using your company's current or quick assets.

2. **Solvency Ratios:** These are also called financial leverage ratios and will compare your company debt levels with your assets, equity and earnings to evaluate whether you can stay afloat in the long-term by paying the long-term debts and interest on the debts.

3. **Profitability Ratios:** These ratios will show how well your company can generate profits from the operations.

4. **Efficiency Ratio:** These are also known as activity ratios and will evaluate how well your company uses its assets and liabilities to generate sales and maximize profits.

5. **Coverage Ratios:** These ratios will measure your company's ability to make the interest payments and other obligations that are associated with its debts.

6. **Market Prospect Ratio:** These are the most commonly used ratios with fundamental analysis. Investors will use these ratios to determine what they may receive in earnings from their investments and to predict what the trend of a stock will be in the future.

Management Information Systems (MIS)

Computers and technology have hit the world by a storm. This is true with the world of accounting as well. I am referring to the Management Information System (MIS). This is a computer-based system that will provide managers with tools to organize, evaluate and efficiently manage departments within your business. This system will use the information from technology through the people and businesses who is it to process and record and also store data that will produce information - to your key decision makers such as the management team - which will be used for the day to day decision-making. It will consist of hardware, a system, the procedures and the people working together. There are some very good reasons for needing this system such as:

➢ **Decision makers will need the information to make the most effective decisions:** MIS makes this possible.

➢ **Your MIS system will facilitate the communication that is outside and within your business:** Employees within your business can easily access the required information they need for the daily operations. Facilities systems like a Short Message Service (SMS) and Email are making it possible for the line of communication to be within your suppliers and customers support channel. This is possible through your MIS systems your business is using.

➢ **Record Keeping:** Your system for your management information will record all the transactions of your business and provides great reference points for each transaction.

What are some of the major components of your MIS system? It is important to know what these components are, so I have included a list of the major components.

➢ **People:** These are the individuals that will use this information system.

➢ **Data:** This will be the data your system will record.

➢ **Business Procedures:** These are the procedures that will be put in place; telling you how to store and analyze the data and record the transactions.

- ➤ **Hardware:** This will usually involve your workstations, printers, equipment for networking and your servers.

- ➤ **Software:** Every business will need to use some type of software. These programs will be used for handling and managing your business data. They will usually involve programs like databases and Spreadsheets.

Different Categories of the Information Systems

The level of your business will decide the information system you will use. There are three levels of users that are major players in your typical business, such as operational management, tactical management and strategic management.

As you look at the diagram, you will see the three major structures. On one side you will notice the decision structure for each level. On the other side, you will also notice the information system each level uses. This is the side we will be talking about. If you noticed, the MIS is the second level with tactical management. However, I am going to briefly mention each one as your business may have different levels and could be using any of these systems.

Transaction Processing Systems (TPS): You will use this system for recording your daily transactions, such as using your Point of Sale (POS) system. This POS system can record your daily sales. This system is at the management level of operational.

Management Information Systems (MIS): These are used as a guide for tactic managers in making important decisions that are semi-structured. The output with these transactions are through process systems that are used for the inputs to your system. The MIS system is used in the tactical management level.

Decision Support Systems (DSS): These will be used with your managers at the top-level for them to make decisions that are semi-structured. Through this output with the MIS systems, they will be transmitted to the DSS systems and the DSS systems will get the data inputs from an external source like the competition, or forces from the current market. The DSS system is used in the strategic support system.

You may have noticed something about these systems. They all work together. For example, the TPS system will transmit data to the MIS system. Then the MIS system will transmit its data to the DSS system.

Advantages and Disadvantages

You will find there will always be advantages and disadvantages to anything you do within your business. The MIS system is no exception. Here are a few of the benefits of having an information system that is computerized:

> ➤ **A Data Processing Retrieval System that is Fast:** This will be the most significant advantages of your MIS being computerized. If you have been in business for a while, you would understand what I am talking about. It was so time-consuming to do all this manually. We can now process data and retrieve this information at a higher rate of speed. This is

great as it will improve your client or customer service experience.

➢ **Data Accuracy Will be Improved:** It is now easier to implement your validation for data and your checks for verification when it is computerized as the computer can help you.

➢ **Security is Improved:** Your business probably already has restricted access to some areas like the database server; however, in addition to that you can equip other forms of controls in security like the control rights of your access, your system for biometric authentication and your user authentication.

➢ **Data Duplication is Reduced:** Your database systems will be designed to minimize duplicate entries. Which means your data that is updating from one of your departments will automatically be available for all departments to view.

➢ **Your System for Backing Up Data is Improved:** Through modern technology, your backup will now be based on the cloud and will make it easier for recovering your data when something happens with your hardware or software that was used to collect your data.

➢ **Your Information is Easy to Access:** Several executives from businesses will be required to make decisions while they are traveling for your business during the time they are not at the main office. Thanks to mobile technologies and the use of the world wide web, it now makes it easy to access your business data while traveling abroad.

Granted, there will be some disadvantages as well:

➢ **It Can Be Expensive for the Set Up and Configure:** You will need to buy the hardware and all the software that is required for running your information systems. You will also need to add business procedures that must be adjusted and you will need to train your staff on how to use the new system.

> **Technology Will be a Heavy Reliance:** Imagine if something was to happen to your software or hardware and all the functions stop with the system. You will not be able to access the data until the system is fixed or replaced which will add an additional cost.

> **There is Risk for Fraud:** When you do not have the correct controls in place, it may leave your system open to intruders who can make transactions that are unauthorized such as goods that are not delivered, and you now have an invoice for those good.

Traits of MIS Professionals: There are a lot of different profiles for an MIS professional. However, I have broken it down to a few traits that make a great MIS professional.

> A good problem solver
> Likes to work with people
> Can think strategically about technology
> Likes responsibility for developing and then implementing their ideas
> Can bridge both the technology and your business
> Can see both details and the big picture
> Are excellent communicators
> Can manage time and resources well

Improved Decision-Making: The purpose of an MIS is for improved decision-making. It does this through up-to-date and accurate data on a variety of organizational assets such as:

> Financials
> Inventory

- ➢ Personnel
- ➢ Project timelines
- ➢ Manufacturing
- ➢ Real estate
- ➢ Marketing
- ➢ Raw materials
- ➢ R&D

The MIS will collect the data, store it and make it accessible to your managers who want to analyze the data by running reports.

Key Performance Indicators (KPIs)

These indicators will measure value that demonstrates how effectively your company is achieving your key business objectives. These KPIs are used by organizations to evaluate their success in reaching targets. Each different type will measure success based on specific goals and targets.

Five financial key performance indicators will gauge your business' health. So, what are those five steps?

- ➢ **Step 1:** Establish Your Goals and Objectives
- ➢ **Step 2:** Establish Your Critical Success Factors (CSF) from Your Goals and Objectives
- ➢ **Step 3:** Establish Key Performance Indicator (KPI) from CSF
- ➢ **Step 4:** Collect Measures
- ➢ **Step 5:** Calculate Metrics from Measures

When you take the time to write and develop your KPI, you should consider how the KPI relates to a specific business outcome or objective. These KPIs should not be a standard form that is already done, and you fill in the blanks. To be successful, they need to be customized to your business solutions and developed to help you achieve your goals. To help point you in the right direction here are a few tips:

- ➤ Write a clear objective for your KPI
- ➤ Share your KPI with stakeholders
- ➤ Review your KPI on a weekly or monthly basis
- ➤ Make sure your KPI is actionable
- ➤ Evolve your KPI to fit the changing needs of the business
- ➤ Check to see that your KPI is attainable
- ➤ Update your KPI objectives as needed

Knowing how to create your KPI is great; however, it is useless if you do not know what to do with it once it is created. Measuring and monitoring your business performance is critical, but working on the wrong key performance indicators can be detrimental.

Now what do we do? I don't want you to be focusing on the wrong areas. Let's break it down to the "key" factors. In fact, there are six key factors that I want you to look at. I call them, "The Six Keys to a Successful KPI." Your business should follow these six factors or best practices.

1. **Aligned:** Make sure your KPI is aligned with your strategic goals and objectives of your business.

2. **Attainable:** Your KPI should measure the data that can be easily obtained.

3. **Acute:** Your KPI should keep everyone on the same page and moving in the same direction.

4. **Accurate:** The data flowing into your KPI should be reliable and accurate.

5. **Actionable:** Does your KPI give insight into your business and is actionable?

6. **Alive:** Your business is always growing and changing. Your KPI should evolve with your business.

Financial Modeling

This is a great tool that is built within a business' financial performance for the future forecast in Excel. These forecasts are usually based on your company's archived performance which will require preparing your income statements, balance sheets, statement of cash flows and all supporting schedules. This is considered a 3-statement model. Several other forms of models can be built.

➢ Three Statement Model

➢ Discounted Cash Flow (DFC) Model

➢ Initial Public Offering (IPO) Model

➢ Leveraged Buyout (LBO) Model

➢ Sum of the Parts Model

➢ Consolidation Model

➢ Budget Model

With all these models that can be created, it is important to know what they can be used for. Once you understand their use, then you understand the different models and which one is best for the situation.

➢ Raising Capital (debt and/or equity)

➢ Making Acquisitions (businesses and/or assets)

➢ Growing Your Business Organically (i.e., opening new stores, entering new markets, etc.)

➢ Selling or Divesting assets and business units

➢ Budgeting and Forecasting (planning for the years ahead)

➢ Capital Allocation (priority of which projects to invest in)

➢ Valuing Your Business

Your modeling of the company's finances is a wonderful tool, and it is wise to know what best practices to use to ensure they are used most effectively.

Excels Tricks and Tips: It is highly essential for you to follow the best practices with Excel as you build your model.

> ➢ Eliminate or limit your use of the mouse. When you use shortcuts on your keyboard, it makes the process much faster.

> ➢ You will have different types of inputs and formulas. You will also have hard-codes. My advice is to use colors. For your hard-codes, you can use blue, while the regular inputs will remain black. You can also keep the formulas black.

> ➢ Do not complicate things. Formulas should be simple while breaking down the harder calculations into steps. Not everyone is familiar with formulas; however, most are familiar with basic math, and when you break down complex calculations it makes it easier for everyone to follow.

> ➢ There are classes that you can find that will not cost much for you to get to know the basic functions and formulas in Excel. There are also books available. It is highly beneficial to know the basics at a minimum.

> ➢ There are several types of queries you can perform in Excel. Instead of using VLOOKUP you will want to use MATCH and INDEX for these queries.

> ➢ Scenarios can also be done within Excel. You will want to use the function CHOOSE for these scenarios to be built.

Formatting: It is imperative to have clear and distinguished inputs (assumptions) and outputs (calculations) for your financial model. For example, when you make your inputs in blue and the formulas in black, then you will be able to use some other types of conventions such as borders or shades.

Model Layout and Design: A critical part of the design is your structure. You must structure your model on a design that is logical and easily followed. In essence, it typically means you will build your entire model with one excel worksheet and group the different sections. Your main section should include the following in this order:

> ➢ Assumptions and drivers

> ➢ Income statement

> ➢ Balance sheet

> ➢ Statement of Cash flows

> ➢ Supporting schedules

> ➢ Valuation

> ➢ Sensitivity analysis

> ➢ Chart and graphs

We have been talking a lot about this financial model. I am sure you are wondering how to create or build it. Let me take some time to break it down for you in steps. Remember; even if you follow these steps exactly your model needs to be for your business and will probably have several revisions until you have it the way you need it.

1. Historical Results and Assumptions: All models will start with your company's archived results. This will be where you begin to build your financial model. Look back at the past financial statements for three years and start inputting the data into Excel. Great! Now you can reverse-design your assumptions from the prior periods through calculating everything such as fixed costs, the growth rate for revenues, variable costs, Accounts Payables, gross margins and inventory days. From this point, you will be able to fill in the information for all your assumptions and record them as the forecast period through hard-codes.

2. Start Your Income Statement: Now that you have the assumptions, you will be able to calculate your top portion of the income statement with your revenue, cost of goods sold (COGS), gross profits and all your operating expenses stopping at your Earnings Before Interest, Taxes, Depreciation and Amortization (EBITDA). However, you must wait to finish the calculations of your amortization, taxes, interests and depreciation.

3. Start Your Balance Sheet: Now that you have the top portion of your income statement completed, you have the information needed to start filling out your balance sheet. We will begin with calculating the inventory and your accounts receivables, which are functions of the Cost of Goods Sold (COGS) and your revenues. They are also part of your assumptions for your Account Receivable and your inventory days. Now you can fill in the accounts payable as that is a function of your Cost of Goods Sold (COGS) and Account Payable (AP) days.

4. Build Your Supporting Schedule: If you look at your balance sheet and your income statement, you will notice they are incomplete. We have some areas that still need to be filled in. However, before we can complete these two statements, you will need to build your capital assets schedule such as the Property, Plant & Equipment (PP&E) to include one for your interest and debts. Your schedule for the PP&E will be pulled from your historical period. You will then add capital expenditures while subtracting the depreciation. Your schedule for debt will be pulled from the past period. You will then add your increased debt and take away your repayments. Your interests will be situated on your averages for a debt balance.

5. Complete Your Balance Sheet and Your Income Statement: Great news! Now that your schedules are complete, you have the information you need to finish your balance sheet and your income statement. Let's start with your income statement. You will now link your depreciation with your schedule for PP&E and then link your interest with your schedule for debt. Once those are linked, you will be able to calculate the before-tax earnings, net income and your taxes. Once that is done we can turn to your balance sheet. You will now link your PP&E closing balance and your debt closing balance that is from your schedules. You will complete your shareholder's equity by pulling your closing balance from last year, adding your net income, adding your raised capital and subtracting the dividends and repurchased shares.

6. Building Your Statement of Cash Flows: Just like when you create the standard financial statements in all accounting, the order still applies with your model. Now that you have your balance sheet and your income statement completed, you can construct your statement of cash flows through a reconciliation method. We will start by looking at the net income. You will add back the depreciation while making any adjustments for the changes in the working capital that is noncash, which will result in the cash from your operations. This Cash can be used with the investing for the functions of your capital expenditures with the schedule of your PP&E and the cash inflow from your assumptions from the financing that are set aside to raising the equity and debt.

7. Perform Your DCF analysis: Awesome! You now have the income statement, balance sheet and the cash flow statement completed. You are off to a great start and now over halfway done with your model. It is now time to figure out the performance of your business valuation and the free cash flows. The free cash flow of your business will discount back as of today which will be at the cost of your capital for the firm (it is your rate of return that is required or the opportunity costs).

8. Add Your Sensitivity Analysis and Your Scenarios: Once you are finished with your DCF analysis and your valuation scenarios, it is time to merge the sensitivity analysis and your scenarios into your model. Thus, showing the analysis and how it will determine the value of your business (or another metrics) and how much impact there will be when changes are made based on the underlying presumption. This will be widely useful to assessing your risk of the investment or your purposes for business planning such as wanting to find out if your business needs to raise money when the sales volume begins to drop by y%.

9. Build Your Charts and Graphs: Everyone loves a good chart or graph. You can tell so much about a company by looking at a chart or graph. Having a crystal communication with the results will be something which will separate a good financial analysis from a great one. The most effective ways of showing these results of your financial model are with these wonderful visual aids. Most executives do not have the time or the patience to look at all the inner structures of your model. That is why these charts are more effective.

10. Run a Stress Test and Audit Your Model: Before I started to share these steps, I mentioned that you might need to modify your model until it is right. That is where the last step comes in and turns this 10-step model into an endless loop. It is now time for you to start to run stress tests to the extreme. The object is to put your model through extreme tests to determine if it behaves as you expect it would. It is crucial that you use the tools for auditing for you to ensure it will be accurate with all your Excel formulas and that they are working as they should.

The Balanced Scorecard

The last tool I want to give you is the balanced scorecard (BSC). This is a great strategy executive tool that is used at all levels. It will help your company in the following:

> ➤ **Clarify Strategy:** It will articulate and communicate your business priorities and objectives.

> ➤ **Monitor Process:** It will measure to the extent your priorities and strategic objectives are being delivered.

> ➤ **Define and Manage Action Plans:** You can ensure your business activities and initiatives are in place to deliver your priorities and strategic objectives.

The purpose of using the tool is to reinforce good behaviors in your business by isolating four separate areas that will need to be analyzed. These four areas will include learning and growth, business processes, customers and finance. Each area will obtain information such as objectives, measurements, initiatives and goals that will result from the primary functions of your business. This makes it easier to identify factors that are hindering your business performance and outlines your strategic changes that are tracked by future scorecards.

Chapter 7 – Theory of Constraints

The theory of constraints has stated that systems consist of a choke point which will prevent it from accomplishing its goals. So, what is a choke point? When I first heard about choke point, I imagined a wrestler putting his opponent in the choke hold. Then I found out what the definition was. It is considered a constraint or bottleneck. That does it, a choke hold and choke point have the same concept, which also means it must be managed carefully to make sure it is mostly always operational. If this is not monitored, then your goals will not be met, mainly because this is how no additional throughput would be able to generate unless its capacity of constraint increases.

This theory will completely violate the traditional point of view of running a successful business whereas all your operations will be optimized to the largest possible extent. When looking at the constraints view, you can see the optimizing of all your operations which can only mean it is easier for you to generate more inventory for it to pile up before the bottleneck operation and without your profits increasing. In essence, this will lead to creating more income instead of profits.

Inventory Buffers

This is another great tool that will help you achieve your goal. Start building your inventory buffer in front of your bottleneck operation. This will ensure your buffer is safeguarded against any shortfalls in this flow as parts come from anywhere upstream of your bottleneck and will not hinder the steady process of flow through this constraint. Your inventory buffer may instead waiver in its size as it will be used and replenished.

With the presence of the upstream, your production problems may also be alleviated by installing the extra sprint capacity for its upstream production area.

Sprint Capacity

This capacity is in an exuberant amount of the production capacity which is assembled within the workstations and will be positioned upstream of its constraint operation. It will be needed when this inevitable production starts to fail or is a failure as it has occurred and this flow goes to parts of the bottleneck and has stopped altogether.

During this stoppage, you will see the bottleneck use parts that are in its inventory buffer and soon causing it to be depleted. This extra from the sprint capacity will then be used for producing an extra-large quantity of more parts to replenish the inventory buffer as it prepares for the next time production will have downtime.

The key point I want you to take from all this is regarding the sprint capacity. Your company should always maintain this excess capacity of your upstream work area, instead of paring down for its production capacity to only a level that will just meet the ongoing demands and needs. This means that when you sell off what could appear as excess equipment, then this is not always the best idea.

Chapter 8 – Careers in Management Accounting

We have been talking a lot about managerial accounting and other areas of interest within the accounting field. Now let's look at the different types of careers available. Keep in mind: many of these figures will be location based. For a more accurate picture, you can look at **www.payscale.com**. This information is as of 2018 and amounts are all based on an annual rate.

Corporate Treasurer

Description/Duties: This position will perform the following tasks:

- ➤ Oversee administration of a corporate treasury which will include the cash management, investments and credit.
- ➤ Train and supervise treasury staff.
- ➤ Take measures to mitigate corporate risk.
- ➤ Ensure financial transactions and reporting complies with the company and government regulations.
- ➤ Develop plans outlining company cash and financial needs.

Average Salary: $82,231

Salary Range: $44,979 - $181,504

Bonus Range: $455 - $50,223

Profit Sharing: $10,000

Total Pay Range: $39,715 - $219,766

Chief Financial Officer (CFO)

Description/Duties: This position will perform the following tasks:

> ➢ Provide leadership and coordination in the administrative, business planning, accounting and budgeting efforts of the company.

> ➢ Prepare or direct preparation of financial statements, business activity reports, financial position forecasts, annual budgets and/or reports that are required by regulatory agencies.

> ➢ Develop internal control policies, guidelines and procedures for activities such as budget administration, cash and credit management, and accounting.

Average Salary: $127,848

Salary Range: $70,364 - $212,816

Bonus Range: $2,031 - $65,359

Profit Sharing Range: $201 - $40,059

Commission Range: $343 - $61,277

Total Pay Range: $70,171 - $252,900

Corporate Controller

Description/Duties: This position will perform the following tasks:

> ➢ Develop and coordinate the operational functions of the accounting department.

> ➢ Ensure accurate reporting and conformance to financial policies.

> ➢ Supervise budget preparation and billing.

- ➢ Oversee accounting activities and cash, investment and asset management.

Average Salary: $93,310

Salary Range: $61,988 - $139,947

Bonus Range: $1,223 - $26,150

Profit Sharing Range: $242 - $14,776

Commission Range: $0.00 - $31,500

Total Pay Range: $62,330 - $152,871

Accounting Manager

Description/Duties: This position will perform the following tasks:

- ➢ You will oversee all the business postings and the business maintenance of the accounts in the general ledger, adjustments, accounts payable and the transactions in the payroll.

- ➢ You will provide the analysis for the financial statements which will include the actual budget, monthly income statements, monthly balance sheets and the statement of cash flows which will include the variance analysis from last year.

- ➢ You will assist with the implementation and development of the procedures and policies that are related to the budget, accounting and financial management.

- ➢ You will manage daily activities with the accounting department.

- ➢ You will provide and collect the required information that is needed for giving assistance to auditors and for audit inquiries.

Average Salary: $68,252

Salary Range: $45,949 - $97,150

Bonus Range: $513 - $12,545

Profit Sharing Range: $0.00 - $8,554

Commission Range: $182 - $14,795

Total Pay Range: $43,645 - $101,585

Financial Analyst

Description/Duties: This position will perform the following tasks:

➤ Provide financial analysis support to various areas of the company.

➤ Prepare detailed annual financial budget and monthly financial forecasts.

➤ Assist with preparation of weekly, monthly and quarterly financial analysis schedules of actual vs budget variances.

Average Salary: $58,858

Salary Range: $43,890 - $79,223

Bonus Range: $510 - $10,180

Profit Sharing Range: $98.95 - $7,525

Commission Range: $0.00 - $31,217

Total Pay Range: $42,964 - $83,004

Cost Accountant

Description/Duties: This position will perform the following tasks:

➤ Analyzes monthly and quarterly ledger activities.

➤ Prepares financial audit schedules and reports for management.

➤ Ensures services and processes are following account practices and regulatory requirements.

> Records and reports the cost of manufacturing goods and providing services.

Average Salary: $54,794

Salary Range: $41,012 - $74,692

Bonus Range: $290 - $6,939

Profit Sharing Range: $98.99 - $7,962

Total Pay Range: $39,498 - $75,849

Budget Analyst

Description/Duties: This position will perform the following tasks:

> Review expenditures to ensure compliance within operational and capital budget limits.

> Provide insight to control and budget policies.

> Prepare budgets for departments based on performance, revenue and expenses.

> Perform trending analysis and projections.

> Maintain expense and audit records for inventories and budget balances.

Average Salary: $58,435

Salary Range: $42,779 - $87,189

Bonus Range: $0.00 - $5,930

Profit Sharing Range: $0.00 - $9,899

Total Pay Range: $41,339 - $86,652

Internal Auditor

Description/Duties: This position will perform the following tasks:

> Conduct operational, compliance, financial and SOX audits within an organization.

- ➤ Act as a liaison for audits with internal departments as well as outside auditors.

- ➤ Evaluate and document existing or proposed procedures and controls.

- ➤ Provide management with recommendations for policy, procedure and practice improvements.

Average Salary: $56,250

Salary Range: $41,055 - $78,226

Bonus Range: $295 - $8,334

Profit Sharing: $0.00 - $5,187

Commission: $5,200

Total Pay Range: $37,451 - $79,579

Fixed Assets Accountant

Description/Duties: This position will perform the following tasks:

- ➤ Maintain financial data for all fixed (non-liquid) assets to include requisitions and inventories.

- ➤ Coordinate project approvals and provide quotes on existing fixed assets.

- ➤ Analyze data and create special reports, trend analysis or other reporting.

- ➤ Complete documentation like journal entries, month end analysis, quarterly reports and capital reports.

Average Salary: $53,122

Salary Range: $40,050 - $71,262

Bonus Range: $511 - $5,870

Profit Sharing: $2,000

Total Pay Range: $38,549 - $70,931

Conclusion

Management accounting is an area that any business will benefit from. You took a ride with me throughout this book in hopes to learn more about this form of accounting and what it can do to help you and your business. I hope you found the answers you were looking for.

I showed you the basics to get started and even went in depth in other areas to point you in the right direction. The tools are at your fingertips. Use them and watch your business grow. These same tools are used in my business daily.

Financial management is at the heart of any business. It is one area that can help drive it forward. Your goal is to succeed and financial management is how you do it.

Take the time to use this book as a guide. This journey is not one to be taken lightly. It will guide you through the twists and turns of the canyon of running your business. However, with this book, you will have an excellent navigator to help you get to the end and reap the rewards.

As we go our separate ways on this adventure and wait for the next, I wish you the best with all your business adventures and leave you with one quote by Barry Liber: "Be passionate about the culture and the business, and remain positive because it inspires others."

Check out more books by Greg Shields

ACCOUNTING

THE ULTIMATE GUIDE TO ACCOUNTING FOR BEGINNERS

Learn Basic Accounting Principles

GREG SHIELDS

BOOKKEEPING

THE ULTIMATE GUIDE TO BOOKKEEPING FOR SMALL BUSINESS

GREG SHIELDS

RISK MANAGEMENT

THE ULTIMATE GUIDE TO
FINANCIAL RISK MANAGEMENT
AS APPLIED TO CORPORATE FINANCE

GREG SHIELDS

FINANCIAL
ACCOUNTING

THE ULTIMATE GUIDE TO
FINANCIAL ACCOUNTING FOR BEGINNERS
INCLUDING HOW TO CREATE FINANCIAL STATEMENTS

GREG SHIELDS